JOHN STANLEY

ORGAN VOLUNTARIES

Volume II

Ten Voluntaries

Opus 6

Edited by

Gordon Phillips

ALLE RECHTE VORBEHALTEN · ALL RIGHTS RESERVED

EDITION PETERS

LEIPZIG · LONDON · NEW YORK

JOHN STANLEY
(1713 - 1786)

The Thirty Organ Voluntaries Op. 5-7
in 3 volumes edited by Gordon Phillips

Volume II: Ten Voluntaries Op. 6

The Thirty Organ Voluntaries — Page

- Editions of these Organ Works ... 2
- Forms of Composition ... 2
- Notes on Performance ... 2
- Ornamentation and Interpretation ... 3

Notes on the Voluntaries, Opus 6 ... 3

Comparative Lists of Stops in the Temple Church Organ of Stanley's Time ... 4

Ten Organ Voluntaries Opus 6

- I in D minor—Siciliano—Andante ... 5
- II in A minor—Andante—Allegro ... 8
- III in G minor—Adagio—Allegro moderato ... 12
- IV in F major—Adagio—Andante ... 16
- V in D minor—Adagio—Andante Largo—Moderato ... 20
- VI in D major—Adagio—Andante—Adagio—Allegro moderato ... 25
- VII in G major—Largo—Vivace ... 31
- VIII in A minor—Largo—Vivace ... 34
- IX in E minor—Adagio—Andante ... 38
- X in G minor—Grave—Andante ... 41

JOHN STANLEY
(1713 - 1786)

The Thirty Organ Voluntaries

edited and introduced by Gordon Phillips

Editions of these Organ Works

The first edition of the Thirty Voluntaries was printed for and sold by John Johnson at the Harp and Crown in Cheapside, London. The respective publication dates were Opus 5, 1748; Opus 6, 1752; Opus 7, 1754. The licence granting permission to the composer to publish his music is printed at the beginning of each volume and is as follows:

GEORGE R.

GEORGE the Second, by the Grace of God, King of Great Britain, France, and Ireland, Defender of the Faith, etc. To all to whom these Presents shall come, Greeting. Whereas Our truly and well beloved JOHN STANLEY, Batchelor of Musick, and Organist of St. Andrew's Holbourn, and of the Temple, in Our City of London, hath by his Petition humbly represented unto Us, that he hath with great Study, Labour and Expence, compos'd divers Works, consisting of Vocal and Instrumental Musick, and being desirous to publish the same, and apprehending, that unless he can obtain Our Royal Licence and Protection, other Persons may be induced to print and publish the said Works, and so invade his Property therein, he hath therefore most humbly pray'd Us to grant him Our Royal Licence and Protection for the sole printing and publishing the above-mention'd Works for the Term of fourteen Years, and for prohibiting all and every other Person or Persons from reprinting, abridging, copying out in Writing, or publishing the same, either in the like, or in any other Size or Manner whatsoever, or importing, buying, selling, vending, or uttering any Copy or Copies thereof reprinted or written beyond the Seas: We being willing to give all due Encouragement to this his Undertaking, are graciously pleas'd to condescend to his Request, and We do therefore, by these Presents, so far as may be agreeable to the Statute in that behalf made and provided, grant unto him, the said JOHN STANLEY, his Executors, Administrators, and Assigns, Our Licence for the sole printing and publishing the said Works for the Term of fourteen Years, to be computed from the Date hereof, strictly forbidding all our Subjects within our Kingdoms and Dominions to reprint, abridge, copy out in Writing for Sale, or publish the same, either in the like, or in any other Size or Manner whatsoever, or to import, buy, vend, utter, or distribute any Copy or copies thereof reprinted or written for Sale beyond the Seas, during the aforesaid Term of fourteen Years, without the Consent or Approbation of the said JOHN STANLEY, his Executors, Administrators, or Assigns, under their Hands and Seals first had and obtained, as they will answer the contrary at their Peril, whereof the Commissioners and other Officers of our Customs are to take Notice that due Obedience may be render'd to Our Pleasure herein declar'd. Given at our Court at Kensington, the Twenty-fourth Day of August, 1742, in the Sixteenth Year of our Reign.

By His MAJESTY'S Command.

CARTERET

George II had commenced his reign in 1727. It ended with his death in 1760. Lord John Carteret, afterwards Earl Granville, was his foreign minister and is described in Turberville's *English Men and Manners in the Eighteenth Century* as 'the marvel of his age, the scholar, the orator, whose self-appointed business it was to make kings and emperors, imperious, intemperate, volatile'.

The publisher John Johnson had established himself by 1740 in Cheapside and remained there in premises opposite to the church of St. Mary-le-Bow until his death c. 1762. His widow carried on the business until 1777.

A later edition of the Voluntaries was published by Harrison & Co. No. 18 Paternoster Row, c. 1785. In this edition a revised text corrects many of the mistakes in the earlier Johnson edition. James Harrison set up business as a music publisher in 1779 and specialised in reprints of works by 18th century English composers.

These two editions of Stanley's Voluntaries form the principal source material and have been collated in the preparation of the present volumes.

Forms of Composition

The thirty voluntaries of John Stanley provide examples of several well-defined forms of composition. These are as follows:

1. Cornet Voluntary—slow movement for Diapasons, followed by quick movement for Cornet stop.
2. Trumpet Voluntary—slow movement for Diapasons, followed by quick movement for Trumpet stop.
3. Echo Voluntary—slow movement for Diapasons, followed by quick movement for Cornet or Trumpet stop, alternating with passages on the Echo organ.
4. Full Voluntary—slow introduction, followed by a quicker fugue, both played on the Full organ, and occasionally containing passages for the Echo organ.

In addition to these four main types there are Voluntaries in which use is made of the Swell organ (Op. 5, Nos. I and VIII. Op. 6, Nos. I and V, Op. 7, Nos. IV and VI) or of individual stops: Stopped Diapason, Flute, Vox Humana, Bassoon and Corno (Horn Diapason?).

In short, these voluntaries exploit to the full the resources of the English 18th century organ as Stanley knew it. Each solo stop is treated idiomatically in a way almost unequalled by any other composer except perhaps William Walond, Francois Couperin and Jean Francois Dandrieu, and to a lesser extent, Jacques Boyvin and William Boyce. The musical thought is always of the highest quality, with a never-failing supply of fresh ideas imaginatively treated and often demanding a brilliant manual technique. A study of the specifications of the organs at St. Andrew's, Holborn* and the Temple Church, as Stanley knew them, will enable the performer to understand what stops were available and what was meant by terms such as Full Organ, Cornet, Echo or Swell. It will be noticed that an echo effect in the same tone quality could be obtained. The Cornet and Trumpet could be echoed perfectly. The full organ was a combination of the Great chorus stops with perhaps the addition of the Trumpet. Samuel Wesley, writing a little later, sometimes uses the direction 'Full Organ without the Trumpet'. In no sense of the word was the full organ anything like the similarly-named effect obtainable from many large instruments of today. It had above all clarity and transparency and of course could not be clouded by heavy 16 ft. or even 32 ft. pedal tone. Manual doubles also were almost completely unknown in English organs during Stanley's lifetime. The resources of the instrument as he knew it may be summed up by an extract from the Quarterly Musical Review for 1820 quoted by Pearce in his Notes on English Organs:

'open and stopped diapasons, which are the foundation of the organ, the principal and flute an octave above the diapasons; the twelfth, fifteenth, tierce, sesquialtera, mixture and furniture, which are the harmonics of the note to which they belong; the trumpet, a reed stop of the pitch of the diapason, the clarion an octave above the diapasons, both used in the full organ; the bassoon, hautboy, and vox humana, imitative stops of the pitch of the diapasons, and the great cornet, consisting of five ranks of pipes, viz., Stopped Diapason, Principal, Twelfth, Fifteenth and Tierce, used only as a solo stop.'

Throughout the thirty voluntaries Stanley shows no inclination to strain the resources of the instruments at his disposal. He demands the generally available stops and no more, and he composes a musical texture which can be perfectly rendered within the limitations of the 18th century organ. Indeed it seems likely that the term 'limitations' might have appeared meaningless to one who worked so easily with the materials that came to hand.

Notes on Performance

Organ and harpsichord touch were interchangeable in the 18th century and indeed in the case of a good many performers were probably identical. Stanley's voluntaries were composed for either organ or harpsichord, and the player who has mastered the technique of a detached touch and the ability to articulate will find no difficulty in dealing with these works on either instrument. The principles of articulation may be studied in the writer's *Articulation in Organ-Playing* and will apply particularly to the slow diapason movements where the contrapuntal parts need individualisation. But the rapid passages in the right-hand part of a cornet allegro will gain in effectiveness if there is a sparing use of legato coupling of notes as opposed to an overall use of staccato; the agogic accent which

* See Introduction, Tallis to Wesley No. 11 (H-1713d).

will result from this treatment will help to establish for the listener the position of stresses and relaxations in the rhythmic flow. The lifelessness of continuous legato or staccato should not be tolerated. Moreover, the various degrees of detachment should be exploited to the full. Staccato notes on weak beats of the bar should be shorter than those on strong beats. Anacrusic groups leading to strong beats may consist of well-detached notes in order to throw the stress onto the correct part of the bar and to guard against false accentuation. The cornet movements were evidently played with great liveliness and brilliance by their best exponents, otherwise they would not have aroused the puritanical wrath of the sombre-minded who, by the end of the 19th century, had removed the last vestige of cheerfulness and gaiety from English organs and organ music.

Similar treatment will, of course, be accorded the movements for trumpet, particularly in the fanfare passages and those employing consecutive thirds on the solo reed. Stanley's fugue subjects are always vitally rhythmical and therefore call for the same liveliness of touch. Careful articulation will establish the musical identity of subject and countersubject, heighten the effect of the many stretti, and point an entry after the listener's attention has been momentarily diverted by the sequential delights of a well-played episode.

Simplicity of treatment will enable the music to reveal its complete character—the stylisation and sophistication of the 18th century combined with a directness of utterance and conciseness of expression which Stanley, with consummate craftsmanship, raised to the level of a unique art-form—the English Voluntary.

Ornamentation and Interpretation

The signs for ornaments used by Stanley, with suggested interpretation are as follows:

tr = trill from upper note with or without turn according to length of note.

⁓ = beat (auxiliary note below—main note—auxiliary note—main note).

$\sim$ = four-note turn—commencing with upper note.

// = two-note slide from below on to main note.

⁓ = mordent (main note—auxiliary note below—main note).

the slide upward 🎵 or downward 🎵 on to main note

the small note appoggiatura 🎵 taking half the value of the main note.

The interpretation of the above ornaments is designed to differentiate between the various signs, although it is not beyond the bounds of possibility that sometimes two different signs mean the same ornament. In this connection it should be pointed out that there are no ornaments in Opus 5 apart from the trill sign in Vol. I and Vol. V, and an appoggiatura sign in Vol. IX, while in Opus 6 and 7 there is profuse ornamentation, with all the above signs included. In Opus 7 however the sign ⁓ practically disappears but tr ⁓ and // are used very frequently. An appoggiatura before a note with a trill sign over it probably signifies a leaning-upon the first note (upper note) of the trill.

The addition of ornaments is permissible. Cadential trills; mordents, slides and beats to give accent to important notes; the short trill to embellish passages descending by step, and the turn to embellish passages ascending by step are a few examples of such permissible added ornaments. Also, where a short adagio passage occurs in an Allegro movement—or a pause mark— it would be appropriate for the performer to improvise a short cadenza, which should be stylistically in keeping with the rest of the movement. A simple example is provided by Stanley in the Allegro of Voluntary IX, Opus 5, commencing 18 bars from the end. Opportunities for such improvised cadenzas occur in the quick movements of Vols. IV and VIII, and the slow movement of Vol. IX in Opus 5 and in similar places throughout Opus 6 and Opus 7. The cadential passages at the end of all diapason movements offer opportunities for short cadenzas according to the performer's taste and skill, but they should be relevant and not just displays of finger agility. Neither should the aleatoric anarchy of today be foisted upon the precise and stylised conceptions of a more disciplined age. A course of reading in the social history of 18th century England is probably a far better preparation for the performance of Stanley and his contemporaries than the most profound study of performance traditions culled from continental authorities and hag-ridden by the intervening tyranny of the Viennese classics. The English voluntary is unique. It has no counterpart. Its integrity must be preserved at all costs and the performer can best do this by playing these works according to the composer's text, with a discreet use of added ornament and cadenza, due observance of the indications of registration and tempo, and the conviction that this music communicates as noble a sentiment and as humanistic a spirit as the more pretentious and more highly publicised works of the nineteenth century.

NOTES ON THE VOLUNTARIES, OPUS 6

Voluntary I in D minor—Siciliano—Andante

The Siciliano for Swell is a unique movement in the Voluntaries. In three parts, with the two upper ones forming an imitative duet above a continuo-like bass, the whole presents an unusually contemplative mood for an opening movement. The choice of the swell presumes the use of the swell pedal and, in Stanley's time, and indeed for many years after, the left-hand part would have to be played on another manual which descended below tenor G. The Andante, a dialogue for Echo organ and Vox humana has its counterpart in many movements by Stanley's contemporaries in France. The authentic slurs towards the end imply inequality or the holding-on of the first note of the couple while the second is played.

Voluntary II in A minor—Andante—Allegro

A typical diapason movement in three contrapuntal parts is followed by an equally typical cornet and echo Allegro. The latter contains interesting use of the beat—the English form of the German mordent and the French pincé, which remained in use in England at least to the end of the eighteenth century. As in many other movements of a similar nature the term Adagio occurring towards the end is probably an indication signifying an improvised cadenza, or at least a long accelerating trill.

Voluntary III in G minor—Adagio—Allegro moderato

The first movement follows a similar pattern to that of Voluntary II. The Allegro moderato for Cornet and Echo makes use of the two-stroke ornament characteristic of the English Virginalist School and could, in this context, be interpreted as a two-note slide from below. The German mordent sign is also used and there are interesting written-out cadenzas at bars 16, 36, 91 and 103.

Voluntary IV in F major—Adagio—Andante

A three- and four-part diapason movement is followed by the Andante which is in the form of a dialogue between Corno and Stopped Diapason. Note the staccato dashes at bar 35 in the left-hand part. This sets an articulation pattern for similar passages at bars 52 and 73.

Voluntary V in D minor—Adagio—Andante Largo—Moderato

The Adagio is the usual diapason movement with a notable use of the chord of the Neapolitan Sixth in bars 18 and 20. The Andante Largo (a correct use of the term Andante with a qualifying adjective) is one of the most popular of Stanley's Trumpet movements and has consequently suffered mutilation at the hands of arrangers. In its authentic form, as presented here, it illustrates the effective use of single, double and triple notes on the trumpet stop, a device described and praised by such eighteenth century authorities on organ-playing as Linley, Marsh and Blewitt. This splendid movement should take its place as a worthy companion to the more frequently performed trumpet pieces by Clarke and Purcell. The Moderato again calls to mind similar movements for solo reed and jeux doux in the organ masses of Couperin and other French writers, the only difference being that Stanley had the Swell organ with its advantage of expressiveness as opposed to the unenclosed jeux doux of the French organs. The three repeated notes of the principal theme should be ornamented consistently according to the pattern in bar 11. The whole movement is characterised by masterly development of the thematic material.

Voluntary VI in D major—Adagio—Andante—Adagio—Allegro moderato

The Adagio follows the usual plan for diapason movements, being in three-part counterpoint not developed at any length. The Andante for Trumpet and Echo consists of phrases repeated antiphonally between the two sections of the organ with a short coda for the solo stop. Double-note passages for the trumpet are again a feature. The Adagio is written to be played throughout on the swell. Two parts form a duet over the customary continuo-like bass, which at one point joins in the imitative writing of the upper parts. The final Allegro moderato, again a popular movement, is for Flute and Echo. One of the composer's most charming inspirations, its lyrical melody is perfectly suited to the Flute stop which in the English organs of the period was always at 4 ft. pitch and accompanied by itself.

Voluntary VII in G major—Largo—Vivace

The Largo, a substantial movement for full organ and echo makes effective use of ejaculatory chords. This leads to the Vivace, a brilliant fugue on a striking subject worked out with considerable resource. Brief interludes on the echo organ contrast well with the main sections of the fugue which are for full organ.

Voluntary VIII in A minor—Largo—Vivace

Similar in conception to Voluntary VII, this 'prelude and fugue', however, employs completely different thematic material. A dotted-rhythm motive is used throughout the Largo and this makes even more striking an impact by the use of double-dotting, an effect probably intended by the composer. The subject of the fugue (Vivace) consists of short phrases separated by rests which contrast well with the smoothly flowing added parts. Episodes marked *piano* are probably intended to be played on the echo organ. The fugue concludes with an effective and exciting stretto which is developed sequentially. Unless the movement is commenced on full organ (there is no indication of registration at the beginning of it) the pause in bar 68 provides an opportunity for addition of stops if the player so chooses.

Voluntary IX in E minor—Adagio—Andante

The Adagio for Full Organ is a sombre movement depending for its effect on chains of suspensions accompanied by running quavers in the bass part. A short cadenza may be introduced in the penultimate bar and the whole movement appears to be suitable for ornamental enrichment in all three parts. The Andante, a fugue on a subject containing the falling diminished seventh, used by Handel, Mozart, Eberlin and many other composers, is typical of Stanley's mastery of contrapuntal writing. Beautifully laid out for the keyboard, it not only has a counter-subject of singular attractiveness but it also contains interesting allusions to the Adagio in bars 33 and 39 and an episode ingeniously divided between a soft and loud organ in bars 29–31. It is one of the composer's most consistently worked-out essays in fugal writing and loses nothing by comparison with similar examples by his great contemporary, Handel. This movement, which is marked Vivace in the Reading manuscript at Dulwich College, would seem to be better served by the slower tempo, indicated as above, in the first edition. The indication Full Organ for the first movement would, in the absence of any further instruction, appear to carry over into the Andante.

Voluntary X in G minor—Grave—Andante

This is another Full Organ voluntary with a well-developed opening movement. Halfway through this an imitational figure makes its appearance reminding one of the similar device in J. S. Bach's Fantasia in the same key. The mordent on the first bass note is in the Harrison Edition published about 1785. The Andante, this time a double fugue, the second subject appearing at bar 80 to be very soon combined with the first, is one of the two movements in all thirty voluntaries in two-four time. The first subject is worked in very effective stretto while the second is developed sequentially at some length.

Gordon Phillips

Comparative Lists of Stops in the Temple Church Organ of Stanley's Time built by Bernard Smith, installed in 1684 and finally purchased 1688

Specification given by Bernard Smith, 1688

Great Organ

1	Prestand of mettle		61 pipes	12 foote Tone
2	Holflute of wood and mettle		61 pipes	12 foote Tone
3	Principall of mettle		61 pipes	6 foote Tone
4	Quinta of mettle		61 pipes	4 foote Tone
5	Super octavo		61 pipes	3 foote Tone
6	Cornett of mettle		112 pipes	2 foote Tone
7	Sesquialtera of mettle		183 pipes	3 foote Tone
8	Gedackt of wainescott		61 pipes	6 foote Tone
9	Mixture of mettle		226 pipes	3 foote Tone
10	Trumpett of mettle		61 pipes	12 foote Tone
			948	

Choir Organ

11	Gedackt wainsecott (*sic*)		61 pipes	12 foote Tone
12	Holflute of mettle		61 pipes	6 foote Tone
13	A Sadt of mettle		61 pipes	6 foote Tone
14	Spitts flute of mettle		61 pipes	3 foote Tone
15	A Violl and Violin of mettle		61 pipes	12 foote Tone
16	Voice humane of mettle		61 pipes	12 foote Tone
			366	

Ecchos

17	Gedackt of wood		61 pipes	6 foote Tone
18	Sup. Octavo of mettle		61 pipes	3 foote Tone
19	Gedackt of wood		29 pipes	—
20	Flute of mettle		29 pipes	—
21	Cornet of mettle		87 pipes	
22	Sesqualtera		105 pipes	
23	Trumpett		29 pipes	
			404	

List of stops made by Christopher Schrieder, 1708

Great Organ

Open diapason of mettle in front	60 pipes
Stop diapason of wood and mettle	60 pipes
Princepall of wood and mettle	60 pipes
The Twelfth of mettle	60 pipes
The Fifteenth of mettle	60 pipes
Cornett of mettle	112 pipes
The Sixquialtera of mettle	180 pipes
The Nason of wood	60 pipes
The mixture of mettle	224 pipes
The Trumpet of mettle	60 pipes
	936

Choir Organ

Stop diapason of wood	60 pipes
The Nason of mettle	60 pipes
Princepall of mettle	60 pipes
The fiffteenth Spitzflute taper of mettle	60 pipes
The Crumhorn, cal'd Cremona Stop, of mettle	60 pipes
The Vox humana Stop of mettle	60 pipes
	360

Ecchos

The Nason of wood	58 pipes
Fiffteenth of mettle	58 pipes
The stop diapason of wood	28 pipes
Princepall of mettle	28 pipes
The Cornett of mettle	84 pipes
The Sixquialtara of mettle	96 pipes
Trumpett of mettle	29 pipes
	381

TEN ORGAN VOLUNTARIES Op. 6

VOLUNTARY I

JOHN STANLEY
(edited by Gordon Phillips)

VOLUNTARY II

VOLUNTARY III

VOLUNTARY IV

VOLUNTARY V

VOLUNTARY VI

VOLUNTARY VII

VOLUNTARY VIII

VOLUNTARY IX

VOLUNTARY X